SAINTS OF THE SACRED HEART

SAINTS OF THE SACRED HEART

EMILY JAMINET

Illustrated by TRACY L. CHRISTIANSON

SOPHIA INSTITUTE PRESS
Manchester, New Hampshire

This book is dedicated to all unborn children;
may they be brought into a world full of the
love and warmth of the Sacred Heart!
—E.J.

Cover and interior design by Perceptions Studio.
Cover and interior artwork by Tracy L. Christianson.

Sophia Institute Press
Box 5284, Manchester, NH 03108
1-800-888-9344
www.SophiaInstitute.com

Sophia Institute Press is a registered trademark of Sophia Institute.
hardcover ISBN 979-8-88911-534-2
ebook ISBN 979-8-88911-535-9
Library of Congress Control Number: to come

First printing

"In contemplating the meaning of our lives, perhaps the most decisive question we can ask is, 'Do I have a heart?'"

POPE FRANCIS

DILEXIT NOS (HE LOVED US)

CONTENTS

LETTER TO PARENTS

"Jesus is the only true friend of our hearts."
ST. MARGARET MARY

Dear Parents,

In June 2024, I went to Paray-le-Monial, France, for the feast of the Sacred Heart of Jesus during the 350th Jubilee celebration. I visited St. Margaret Mary and her dear friend Claude de la Colombière in their respective chapels and witnessed firsthand how this remote little town has become the epicenter of Jesus' loving Heart for the whole world.

Jesus' loving Heart is the answer to all the aches, pains, sorrows, and difficulties in our world that impact our families. As parents, we need Jesus to heal our hearts and help us raise our children with the spiritual stability of knowing Jesus' loving Heart. This devotion bears great fruit, and Jesus desires to be our safe refuge.

Devotion to the Sacred Heart brings hope to all families. Jesus wants to renew the face of the earth by allowing His loving Heart to impact each and every heart. If we make room for Jesus, we will truly be meek, humble, and patient, and our homes will be places of charity and peace. Now is the time to embrace Jesus' Heart to see what His perfect love can do and the abundant blessings He desires to pour out in our lives.

During this great Jubilee in 2024, Pope Francis wrote a powerful encyclical letter on the Sacred Heart titled *Dilexit Nos* to help us better love Jesus and care for our hearts, as many have lost their hearts and even lost their way. This letter was written just months before the Jubilee of Hope, which coincides with the 350th Jubilee celebration of the Sacred Heart. I believe these overlapping celebrations point to the significance of Jesus' desire to renew our society through His love, just as He did many years ago, starting with St. Margaret Mary.

In this encyclical, Pope Francis states that the heart is "not only the centre of the body, but also the human soul and spirit". We hold our desires, wishes, concerns, worries, hopes, and dreams in our hearts. As Catholics, we know that our motivation to be great saints or sinners starts in our hearts, with our intentions. While most of us clearly desire to do good, we sometimes must admit suffering from a bit of hard-heartedness. The ten remarkable saints in this book had a particular connection with or devotion to Jesus' loving Heart, and they inspire us and show us how to cultivate more loving hearts and to be more like Jesus!

This book begins with the story of St. Margaret Mary, the Disciple of the Sacred Heart, followed by the stories of nine saints, along with individual reflections and accompanying prayers. If you wish, you can use the prayers at the end of this book to turn your reading experience into a novena (reading about one saint per day for nine days).

When Jesus appeared to St. Margaret Mary, He said that He wanted His holy image exposed and honored so that we might be blessed and understand that His Heart is a place of refuge on our journey toward holiness. Jesus, whose love is eternal and limitless, offers us His love with no conditions, barriers, or restrictions. All we must do is receive it and share it with others, and then we may one day be like the holy friends in these pages: saints in Heaven. I pray that this book may bring you closer to Jesus, closer as a family, and lay the groundwork for a life rooted in His eternal love. May Jesus' eternal love rest with you always!

In Christ's loving Heart,
Emily Jaminet

P.S. Have you invited the Sacred Heart into your heart and your home? If you would like to know more about how to dedicate your home to Jesus through the Enthronement of the Sacred Heart, visit **www.WelcomeHisHeart.com**.

MEET

ST. MARGARET MARY ALACOQUE

DISCIPLE OF THE SACRED HEART, 1647–1690

"Give me a heart of love!"

Just after Christmas in 1673, Jesus appeared to a young religious sister named Margaret Mary Alacoque. She lived in a Visitation convent in the small town of Paray-le-Monial in France.

As she was praying, Jesus appeared to Sr. Margaret Mary and told her a secret: His Heart was on fire with love for all mankind. "Will you be my disciple, a disciple of the Sacred Heart?" He asked her. "Will you share my message of the Sacred Heart?" Jesus wanted *everyone* to know the secrets of His Heart!

"Give me a heart of love!" Sr. Margaret Mary pleaded. And Jesus did. Sr. Margaret Mary soon discovered that the more she responded to Jesus' love and entrusted her heart to Him, the better she was able to love everyone! In this book, we will meet nine of St. Margaret Mary's special friends, who offered themselves to the Sacred Heart and helped to share the message of the Sacred Heart with the whole world.

Have you offered your heart to Jesus, so He can fill it with His love? He wants us to come to Him every day and to offer everything we do and say as a prayer to Him: our joys and trials, our hopes and sufferings. No offering is too small!

One of the secrets Jesus shared with St. Margaret Mary is that He longs to share His love with us in the Holy Eucharist, our spiritual food. He gives us special graces when we make acts of reparation (to make up for sins against God), especially by spending holy hours with Him and receiving Holy Communion on the first Friday of each month. He wants us to put Him at the center of our homes, so that we can always be reminded of His love.

OFFERING OF THE HEART

Does the Sacred Heart of Jesus live in your heart? What keeps you from offering your heart to Jesus?

LET'S PRAY!

Sacred Heart of Jesus Prayer (page 25)

St. Margaret Mary, pray for us!
Help us to be true friends of Jesus!

NOVENA SAINTS & PRAYERS

DAY 1

A HEART OF FRIENDSHIP

MEET

ST. CLAUDE DE LA COLOMBIÈRE, S.J.

PROMOTER AND DEFENDER OF THE SACRED HEART DEVOTION, 1641–1682

"Give me a heart for true friendship!"

After Jesus appeared to St. Margaret Mary Alacoque, telling her the secrets of His Sacred Heart, she began to tell others what Jesus said to her. Some people did not believe her—her claims were so hard to believe! But Jesus sent her a special helper in St. Claude de la Colombière. St. Claude became the personal confessor and spiritual adviser of St. Margaret Mary, helping her to promote and share the Sacred Heart devotion.

St. Claude was a Jesuit priest and a true friend of Jesus; he wanted to please God in his words and actions. He was a great preacher and teacher, yet the Lord sent him to a small corner of France to serve the Visitation sisters. After meeting with St. Margaret Mary, he came to believe the mystical revelations she shared. He told the other sisters that it was okay for them to believe St. Margaret as well.

A short time later, St. Claude was sent to London, where he continued to live out the devotion to the Sacred Heart and encouraged everyone to trust in Jesus. He was later persecuted for his faith, even being sent to prison. After he was freed, he returned to that small town in France for the remainder of his life. He was buried down the street from his friend St. Margaret Mary Alacoque. They now spend eternity in Heaven together.

OFFERING OF THE HEART

Do you have a friend you can share your faith with?
Have you considered praying for God to send you a true
friend, as St. Claude was for St. Margaret Mary?

LET'S PRAY!

Sacred Heart of Jesus Prayer (page 25)

St. Claude de la Colombière, pray for us!
Help us to be true friends of Jesus!

DAY 2
A HEART FOR THE SUFFERING

MEET

ST. GERTRUDE THE GREAT

A SAINT FULL OF COMPASSION AND LOVE, 1256–1301

"Teach us to have a heart for the suffering."

St. Gertrude the Great, another friend of the Sacred Heart, was a German Benedictine nun and mystic who loved Jesus with her whole heart. She was known for her deep spiritual writings and her devotion to the Sacred Heart of Jesus long before this devotion became popular.

One day, St. Gertrude had a very special mystical experience in which Jesus invited her to rest her head on His chest and listen to His heartbeat. Just imagine what that must have been like, to rest your head on Jesus' chest! Every day, Jesus invites us to listen to Him and draw closer to His Heart by praying and asking Him for more graces. When we take the time out of our busy lives to pray, we can be more like Jesus and share His love with others through our prayers and deeds.

St. Gertude had compassion for the suffering, especially the holy souls suffering in Purgatory. Here is her special prayer for them: "Eternal Father, I offer You the Most Precious Blood of Your Divine Son, Jesus, in union with the Masses said throughout the world today, for all the holy souls in Purgatory, for sinners everywhere, for sinners in the universal Church, those in my own home, and within my family. Amen."

Gertrude encouraged others to honor and pray to the Sacred Heart of Jesus. Jesus told her, "They [meaning all of us] may draw forth all they need from my Divine Heart." Let's be a friend of Gertrude, and pray for those who are hurting, especially those who have died. When we combine our prayers with our actions, we become beacons of light, love, and comfort to others.

OFFERING OF THE HEART

Can you think of any friends or family members who have died and need your prayers? How can we show kindness and compassion to those in need?

LET'S PRAY!

Sacred Heart of Jesus Prayer (page 25)

St. Gertrude the Great, pray for us!
Help us to be true friends of Jesus!

DAY 3

A HEART FOR EVERY-DAY HOLINESS

MEET

ST. FRANCIS DE SALES

DOCTOR OF LOVE, 1567–1622

"Be who you are and be that well."

St. Francis de Sales taught that every person can be holy. This friend of the Sacred Heart was a priest, a bishop, and a Doctor of the Church. He understood the importance of the heart and its relationship to God. He wrote, "Only in the fully divine and fully human Heart of Jesus is love perfected." His preaching and teaching brought many Catholics back to the Faith.

In 1610, St. Francis de Sales and his friend St. Jane de Chantal started the Visitation Order, the religious community that St. Margaret Mary would later join. God inspired

St. Francis to select, as a symbol of the order, the Heart of Jesus with the crown of thorns around it. The order's motto is "Live Jesus."

The sisters embraced a beautiful life of prayer and work and were known for their humility and gentleness. When they started the order, St. Francis wrote to St. Jane, "My advice is that henceforth we live no more in ourselves, but that in heart, intention, and confidence we lodge forever in the pierced side of the Savior." St. Francis invites us to do the same, as we learn to trust in Jesus and seek to do His will each day.

OFFERING OF THE HEART

Imagine if your family were to "live Jesus," and everyone was gentle and humble. Jesus tells us, "Learn from me; for I am gentle and lowly in heart, and you will find rest for your souls" (Matt. 11:29). Serving others with humility and gentleness is a beautiful way to transform your heart and your home! What are some ways you can do that?

LET'S PRAY!

Sacred Heart of Jesus Prayer (page 25)

St. Francis de Sales, pray for us!
Help us to be true friends of Jesus!

DAY 4

A MISSIONARY HEART OF SERVICE

MEET

ST. MARTIN DE PORRES

A DOMINICAN BROTHER OF CHARITY, 1579–1639

"Everything … could be a prayer, if it were offered to God."

This saint of the Sacred Heart was known by all who knew him as "Martin of Charity." Martin had a difficult life as a child. He was born in Peru to a Spanish nobleman and a woman who was a freed slave from Panama. When his father left his family in horrible poverty, Martin was often teased and mistreated because of his skin color and his family situation. Amazingly, he allowed these hardships to bring him closer to Jesus.

Martin was known for his deep devotion to the Passion of the Lord, in which the love of Jesus' Heart was poured out for the whole world. At the age of fifteen, Martin was accepted as a volunteer at the Dominican abbey in Lima, Peru. He spent his life cutting hair, helping and tending to the sick, answering the door, cleaning, and, of course, praying! He treated everyone with dignity and respect, no matter what. When others were mean to him, he responded with love and kindness. At age twenty-four, Martin was given special permission to join the Third Order of St. Dominic. He worked in the abbey's infirmary, the place for the sick and the dying, until his death at the age of sixty.

Despite the difficulties he experienced in life, Martin always served others with the love of Christ in his heart. Once he got in trouble for tending the sick instead of observing the friary's community routine. He responded, "Forgive me. I did not know that obedience was more important than charity." After that, he was given permission to give priority to acts of mercy and kindness over following the community routine.

OFFERING OF THE HEART

St. Martin de Porres, the first Black saint of the Americas, is an inspiration because he was always kind and virtuous. He is believed to have worked many wonderful miracles and healings attributed to his deep faith. How can you be more like St. Martin de Porres in your family?

LET'S PRAY!

Sacred Heart of Jesus Prayer (page 25)

St. Martin de Porres, pray for us!
Help us to be true friends of Jesus!

MEET

ST. LOUIS DE MONTFORT

MISSIONARY APOSTOLIC WHO LOVED MARY, 1673–1716

"Totus tuus [Totally yours]."

St. Louis-Marie Grignion de Montfort is a special saint who always had a deep devotion to the Eucharist, to the Blessed Mother, and to the Holy Rosary. This friend of the Sacred Heart took the name Marie at his Confirmation to honor the Blessed Mother, and he spent his life working hard to help Catholics experience the love of Christ through Mary. He said, "Mary is the safest, easiest, shortest, and most perfect way of approaching Jesus."

St. Louis de Montfort became a priest at the age of twenty-seven. At that time, the spread of a bad teaching was causing confusion among the faithful, making them feel unworthy of Jesus' love. Fr. de Montfort spent many years encouraging people to return to Jesus—by getting closer to His Mother. Mary always leads us to Jesus, and Jesus desires us to encounter His wonderful Mother.

We know that Mary is the Mother of God and that her heart is a perfect vessel of love that was never stained with sin. Her Immaculate Heart is perfect and full of love for us. St. Louis de Montfort wanted others to know about Mary and the beautiful intercessor she is for all of us. Despite Mary's difficult sorrows, which hurt her heart and made her sad at times, she always responded with love and service to God.

OFFERING OF THE HEART

The Immaculate Heart image shows Mary's heart encircled by beautiful roses, with a sword piercing it (to represent her sorrows). How can your heart be more like Mary's heart? How can you better honor the Blessed Mother today?

LET'S PRAY!

Sacred Heart of Jesus Prayer (page 25)

St. Louis de Montfort, pray for us!
Help us to be true friends of Jesus and Mary!

DAY 6

A HEART FOR GOD'S WAYWARD CHILDREN

MEET

ST. JOHN BOSCO

PATRON SAINT OF SCHOOLCHILDREN, 1815–1888

"Act today in such a way that you need not blush tomorrow."

St. John Bosco was born in 1815 into a poor farming family in Becchi, Italy. Early on, he wanted to be a priest, but he had to grow up quickly when his father died. He left home at the age of twelve to work on a farm to help support his family and learned some acrobatic acts from a traveling circus. When he finally did become a priest, with the help of a priest who paid for his education, these talents came in handy when he wanted to share the gospel with children.

Don Bosco had a special place in his heart for young children and teens due to his experiences as a youth; he knew what to do when they were struggling and even rebelling against God: He would seek them out and try to bring them to the loving Heart of Jesus! During his life, he helped find housing for more than eight hundred boys, and he also helped boys find work that was safe and fair. St. John Bosco saw how important children are in the kingdom of God.

In 1859, Fr. Bosco established the Society of St. Francis de Sales, also known as the Salesians. Fr. Bosco promoted devotion to Jesus' loving Heart by commissioning the Basilica of Our Lady Help of Christians in Turin, Italy. He always fostered a culture of love and mercy among youth, reflecting the love of Christ's Heart to the world.

OFFERING OF THE HEART

How can you help those you meet who are struggling—at school, in the neighborhood, or in your community? In what ways can you bring Christ's love to those who do not know and love Him?

LET'S PRAY!

Sacred Heart of Jesus Prayer (page 25)

St. John Bosco, pray for us!
Help us to be true friends of Jesus!

MEET

ST. FRANCES XAVIER CABRINI

ADVOCATE FOR IMMIGRANTS AND CHILDREN, 1850–1917

"I will ... do anything in order to communicate the love of Jesus to those who do not know Him or have forgotten Him."

This special friend of the Sacred Heart, Mother Cabrini, is a remarkable example of how one person can make a difference in the world when he or she puts Christ first. Born in Italy as the youngest of thirteen children, young Frances always had a deep love for Christ and the Catholic Church. Despite her delicate health, her dream was to go to China and share the gospel.

Determined not to let her health stop her, she started a missionary order, the Missionary Sisters of the Sacred Heart, and went to the pope to ask permission to take her sisters to the Far East. But God had other plans! Pope Leo XIII told her she was to go "not to the East, but to the West." He wanted Mother Cabrini and her sisters to go to America, to care for the poor Italian immigrants living there.

Mother Cabrini arrived in New York in 1889, shocked to witness the suffering and poverty of the Italian immigrants. She and her sisters got to work, reciting the Bible verse that had become their motto: "I can do all things in Him who strengthens me" (Phil. 4:13). They started schools, orphanages, and even a hospital for the needy. They shared Jesus with everyone through kindness, care, and compassion. After twenty years in America, Mother Cabrini became a U.S. citizen.

During the investigation for her canonization, it was discovered that her heart was incorrupt; it did not decompose in death because, during her life, she had a mystical "exchange of hearts" with Jesus. On the day of her canonization, more than forty-five thousand people came to venerate her relics. Mother Cabrini was the first American to be canonized, and she is the universal patroness of immigrants.

OFFERING OF THE HEART

How can you teach someone about the love of the Sacred Heart? Have you ever thought of being a missionary, either overseas or right at home? What is one thing you can do today to help solve the problems in your community and your country?

LET'S PRAY!

Sacred Heart of Jesus Prayer (page 25)

St. Frances Xavier Cabrini, pray for us!
Help us to be true friends of Jesus!

DAY 8

A HEART PIERCED BY LOVE

MEET

ST. PIO OF PIETRELCINA (PADRE PIO)

ITALIAN CAPUCHIN CONFESSOR AND MIRACLE WORKER, 1887–1968

"Pray, hope, and don't worry."

St. Padre Pio, a Capuchin mystic and saint of the Sacred Heart, followed the way of St. Francis of Assisi. Like St. Francis, St. Pio lived in a small town in Italy and changed the world by how he lived out his vocation and his deep love for Christ.

From the time he was five years old, young Francesco (his given name) dedicated his life to Christ. Joining the Capuchin community, a branch of the Franciscan Order, while still a teenager, he was so tenderly pierced by the love of Christ that, when he became a priest, many traveled from all corners of the world just to attend a Mass offered by him, to confess their sins to him, or to pray with him. Padre Pio recited the Sacred Heart Novena daily for those who requested his prayers (see page 25).

St. Padre Pio was known for being a miracle worker and had the stigmata (the wounds of Christ), just like St. Francis of Assisi. He was also known to bilocate (be in two places at the same time). Demons hated him because he was so holy. This great saint spent many hours a day in the confessional, listening to others and offering them forgiveness and encouragement. It was said that he could read the hearts of people and tell them their sins so that they could change their ways. Jesus doesn't want us to hide from Him but, rather, to run to His loving arms so He can remove our worries and anxiety and fill us with peace.

OFFERING OF THE HEART

Padre Pio is a powerful example of how the Lord desires to change our hearts and allow His love to fill us in the Sacrament of Reconciliation. When was the last time you went to Confession? Do you need to go again?

LET'S PRAY!

Sacred Heart of Jesus Prayer (page 25)

St. Padre Pio, pray for us!
Help us to be true friends of Jesus!

DAY 9
A HEART FULL OF DIVINE MERCY

MEET

ST. FAUSTINA KOWALSKA

APOSTLE OF DIVINE MERCY, 1905–1938

"Jesus, I trust in You."

Now we come to the last friend of the Sacred Heart in this book: St. Faustina Kowalska. She was the third of ten children born in Poland to a poor, religious family of peasants. Her parents called her Helen. She teaches us that Our Lord often loves to use the small, lowly, and faithful to share His Kingdom of love.

St. Faustina is known as the Apostle of Divine Mercy because Jesus appeared to her and invited her to share the message of Divine Mercy with the world. He wants all of us to know that we should trust in Him and be open to receiving His mercy. That mercy is a gift. You don't have to earn it. All you need to do is ask for it!

When St. Faustina was a religious sister, Jesus appeared to her and instructed her to commission the Divine Mercy image, which shows rays of love and mercy flowing from His Heart. At the bottom of the image are the words "Jesus, I trust in You." Jesus asked St. Faustina to promote the Divine Mercy Chaplet, in which we pray for mercy "on us and on the whole world." Jesus also asked that the Sunday after Easter be known as the feast of Divine Mercy. Jesus wants the whole world to know about the infinite mercy of God.

OFFERING OF THE HEART

What are some ways the Lord shows His mercy and love to you? Have you ever seen His mercy change someone's heart? How can you be more prayerful and merciful at home?

LET'S PRAY!

Sacred Heart of Jesus Prayer **(page 25)**

St. Faustina, pray for us!
Help us to be true friends of Jesus!

ADDITIONAL PRAYERS

SACRED HEART OF JESUS PRAYER

If you wish, offer this short prayer at the conclusion of each story before you read the "Let's Pray" section.

Lord, make our family a holy family. Let Your love spring up from our hearts and heal us from the inside out. Strengthen our relationships, comfort us when we feel pain, and bring us graces when we need them. Lord, fill us with Your peace, love, hope, and charity. Help us to forgive those who have hurt us; help us to be a shining light to those who do not know You, Jesus. May we always rejoice in Your love.

Lord, I offer this intention in this novena: (*state your intention*). Amen.

ST. MARGARET MARY'S NOVENA PRAYER

Although this novena is traditionally offered for nine days prior to the Solemnity of the Most Sacred Heart, you can offer it anytime!

To receive special graces as you pray this novena, consider going to confession together and receiving Jesus in the Eucharist.

✠ In the name of the Father, and of the Son, and of the Holy Spirit. Amen.

PRAYER ONE

O my Jesus, You have said: "Truly I say to you, ask and you will receive, seek and you will find, knock and it will be opened to you." Behold, I knock, I seek, and I ask for the grace of (*name your request and then offer one Our Father, one Hail Mary, and one Glory Be*):

> *Our Father who art in Heaven, hallowed be Thy Name; Thy Kingdom come; Thy will be done on earth as it is in Heaven. Give us this day our daily bread, and forgive us our trespasses, as we forgive those who trespass against us, and lead us not into temptation, but deliver us from evil. Amen.*

Hail Mary, full of grace, the Lord is with thee. Blessed art thou amongst women, and blessed is the fruit of thy womb, Jesus. Holy Mary, Mother of God, pray for us sinners, now and at the hour of our death. Amen.

Glory be to the Father, and to the Son, and to the Holy Spirit, as it was in the beginning, is now, and ever shall be, world without end. Amen.

Sacred Heart of Jesus, I place all my trust in You. Amen.

PRAYER TWO

O my Jesus, You have said: "Truly I say to you, if you ask anything of the Father in my name, He will give it to you." Behold, in Your name, I ask the Father for the grace of (*name your request and then offer one Our Father, one Hail Mary, and one Glory Be*):

Our Father who art in Heaven, hallowed be Thy Name; Thy Kingdom come; Thy will be done on earth as it is in Heaven. Give us this day our daily bread, and forgive us our trespasses, as we forgive those who trespass against us, and lead us not into temptation, but deliver us from evil. Amen.

Hail Mary, full of grace, the Lord is with thee. Blessed art thou amongst women, and blessed is the fruit of thy womb, Jesus. Holy Mary, Mother of God, pray for us sinners, now and at the hour of our death. Amen.

Glory be to the Father, and to the Son, and to the Holy Spirit, as it was in the beginning, is now, and ever shall be, world without end. Amen.

Sacred Heart of Jesus, I place all my trust in You. Amen.

PRAYER THREE

O my Jesus, You have said: "Truly I say to you, heaven and earth will pass away, but my words will not pass away." Encouraged by your infallible words, I now ask for the grace of (*name your request and then offer one Our Father, one Hail Mary, and one Glory Be*):

Our Father who art in Heaven, hallowed be Thy Name; Thy Kingdom come; Thy will be done on earth as it is in Heaven. Give us this day our daily bread, and forgive us our trespasses, as we forgive those who trespass against us, and lead us not into temptation, but deliver us from evil. Amen.

Hail Mary, full of grace, the Lord is with thee. Blessed art thou amongst women, and blessed is the fruit of thy womb, Jesus. Holy Mary, Mother of God, pray for us sinners, now and at the hour of our death. Amen.

Glory be to the Father, and to the Son, and to the Holy Spirit, as it was in the beginning, is now, and ever shall be, world without end. Amen.

Sacred Heart of Jesus, I place all my trust in You. Amen.

CONCLUDING PRAYER

O Sacred Heart of Jesus, for whom it is impossible not to have compassion on the afflicted, have pity on us miserable sinners and grant us the grace that we ask of You, through the Sorrowful and Immaculate Heart of Mary, Your tender Mother and ours.

Hail, Holy Queen, Mother of Mercy, our life, our sweetness, and our hope. To thee do we cry, poor banished children of Eve. To thee do we send up our sighs, mourning and weeping in this valley of tears.
Turn then, most gracious advocate, thine eyes of mercy toward us, and after this our exile show unto us the blessed fruit of thy womb, Jesus.

O clement, O loving, O sweet Virgin Mary.

Pray for us, O holy Mother of God that we may be made worthy of the promises of Christ.

St. Joseph, foster father of Jesus, pray for us. Amen.

✠ In the name of the Father, and of the Son, and of the Holy Spirit. Amen.

ABOUT THE AUTHOR AND ILLUSTRATOR

EMILY JAMINET

is a celebrated author, speaker, and mother of seven, dedicated to enriching family life through faith and service. She is currently the national executive director at the Sacred Heart Enthronement Network, where she promotes devotion to the Sacred Heart and teaches families how to make this powerful devotion a cornerstone of their domestic church.

TRACY L. CHRISTIANSON

is a talented artist and designer whose collection (PortraitsofSaints.com) contains exquisite portraits of more than 650 saints.

ABOUT SOPHIA INSTITUTE

Sophia Institute is a nonprofit institution that seeks to nurture the spiritual, moral, and cultural life of souls and to spread the gospel of Christ in conformity with the authentic teachings of the Roman Catholic Church.

Sophia Institute Press fulfills this mission by offering translations, reprints, and new publications that afford readers a rich source of the enduring wisdom of mankind.

Sophia Institute also operates the popular online resource CatholicExchange.com. *Catholic Exchange* provides world news from a Catholic perspective as well as daily devotionals and articles that will help readers to grow in holiness and live a life consistent with the teachings of the Church.

In 2013, Sophia Institute launched Sophia Teachers to renew and rebuild Catholic culture through service to Catholic education. With the goal of nurturing the spiritual, moral, and cultural life of souls, and an abiding respect for the role and work of teachers, we strive to provide materials and programs that are at once enlightening to the mind and ennobling to the heart; faithful and complete, as well as useful and practical.

Sophia Institute gratefully recognizes the Solidarity Association for preserving and encouraging the growth of our apostolate over the course of many years. Without their generous and timely support, this book would not be in your hands.

www.SophiaInstitute.com
www.CatholicExchange.com
www.SophiaTeachers.org